# ANIMAL MANDALA
## ADULT COLORING BOOK

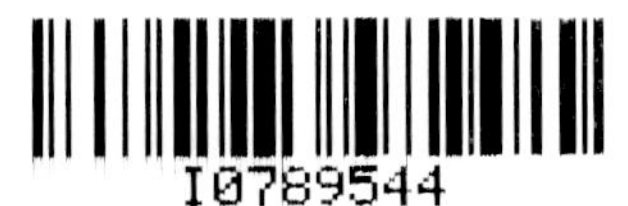

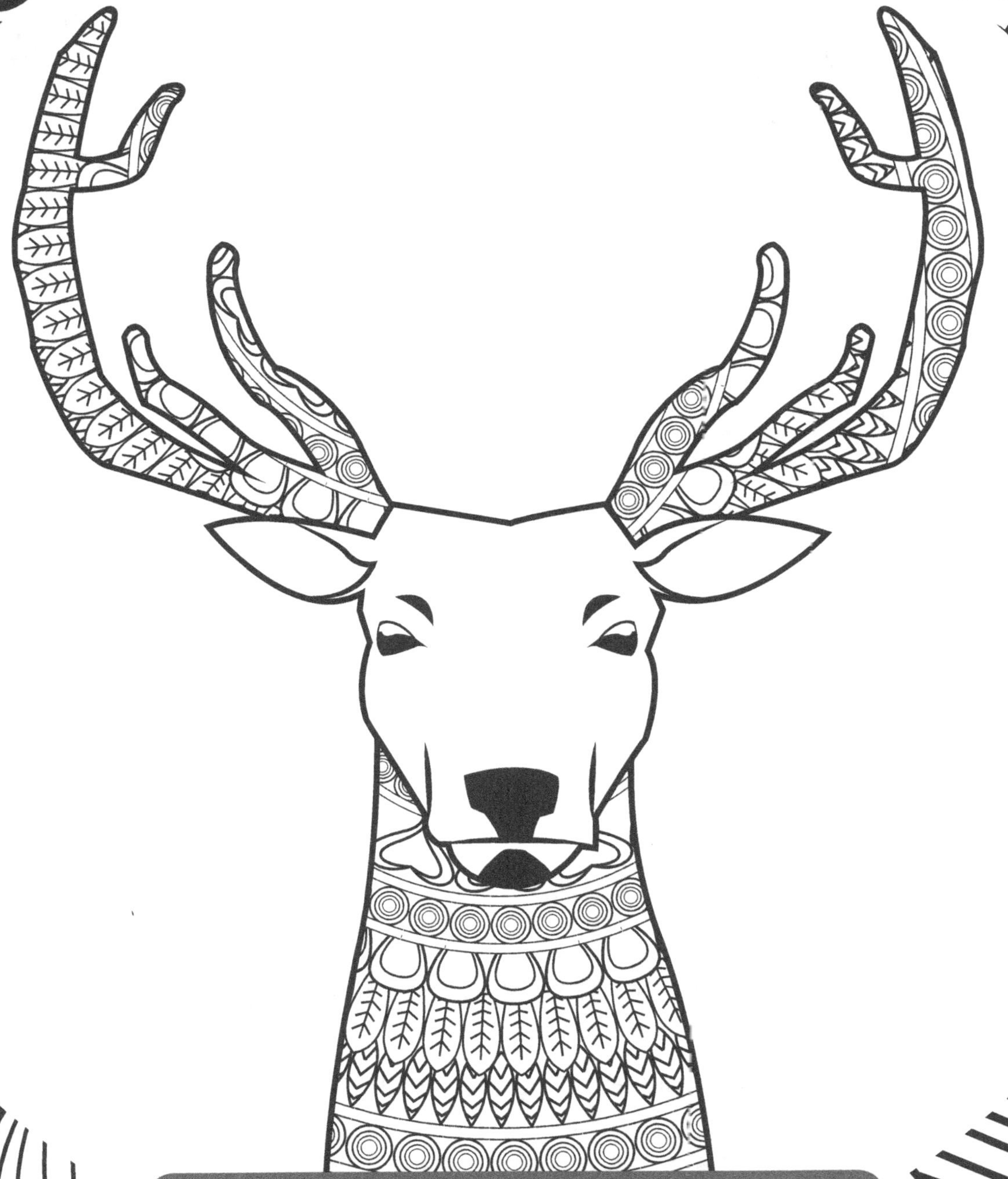

**ANIMALS, MANDALAS, FLOWERS, PAISLEY PATTERNS**

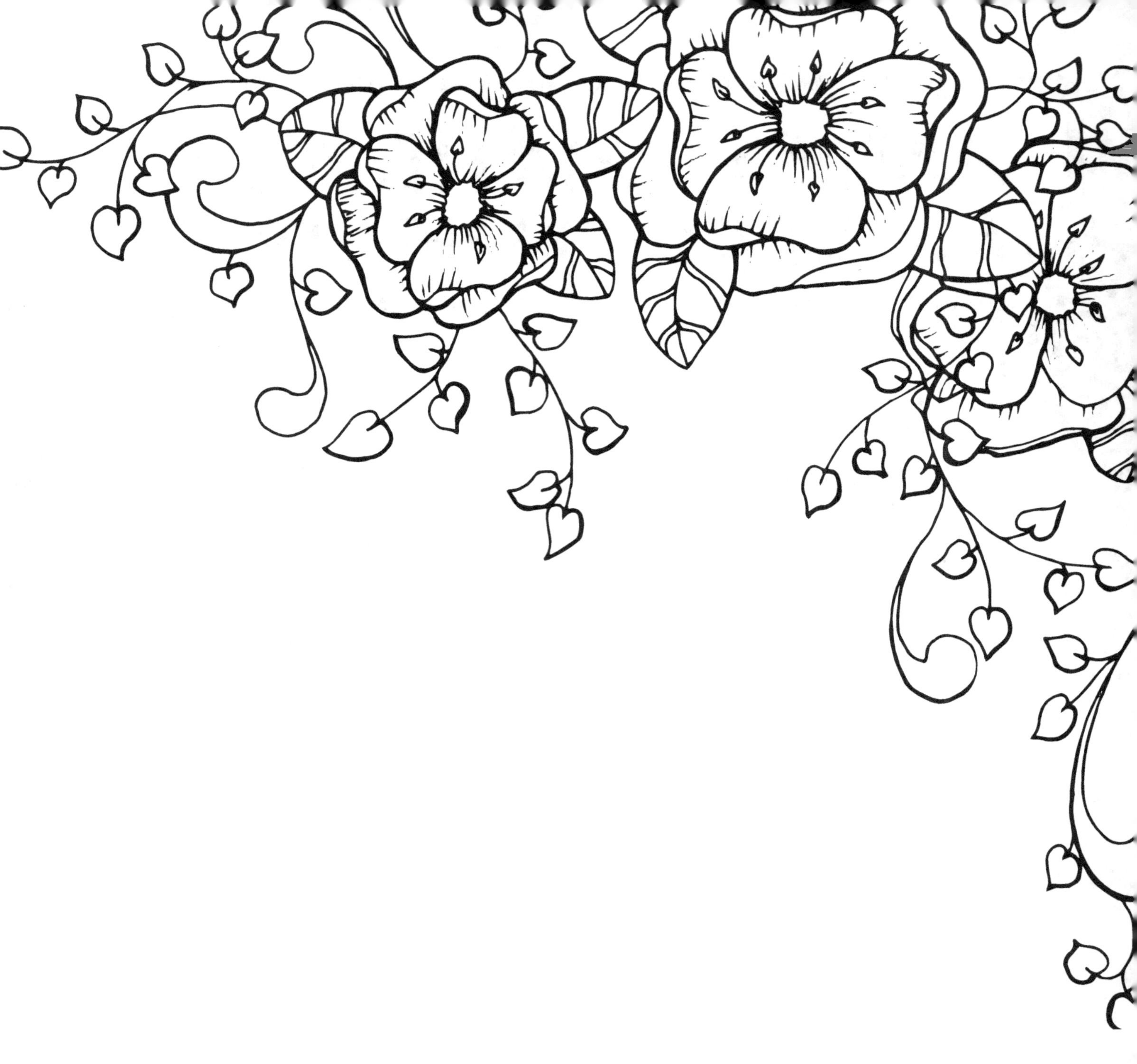



ISBN: 9798706468309

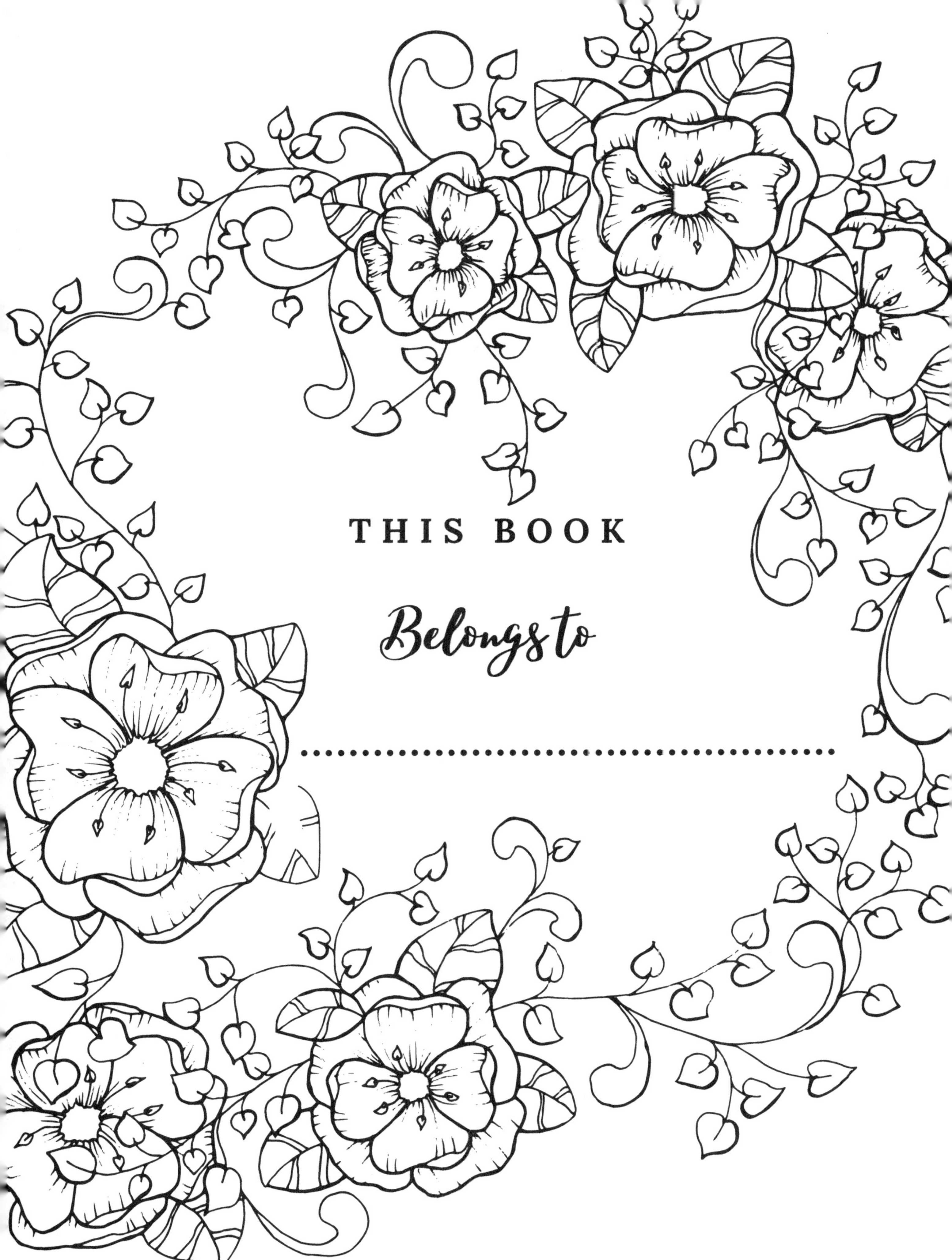

THIS BOOK

Belongs to

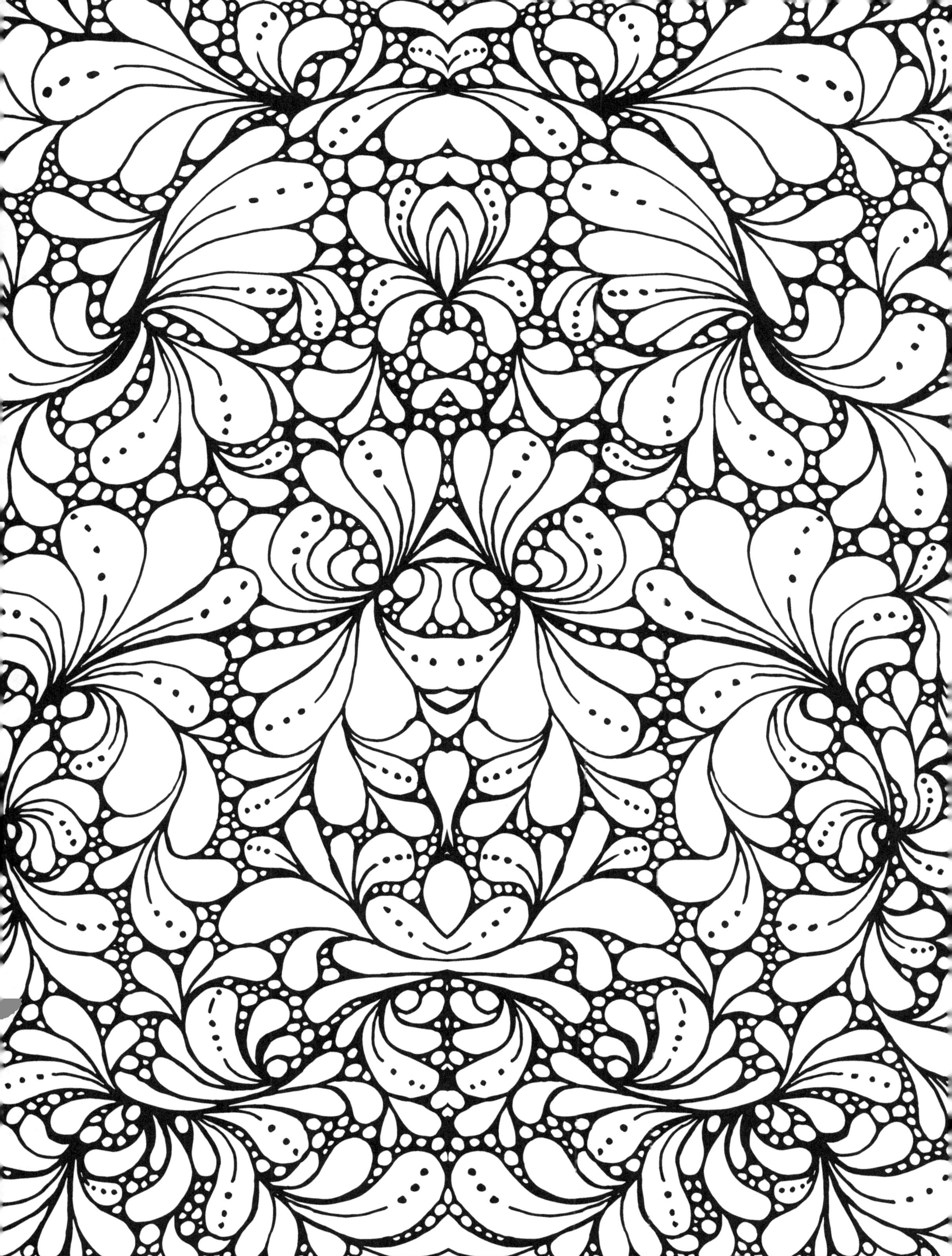

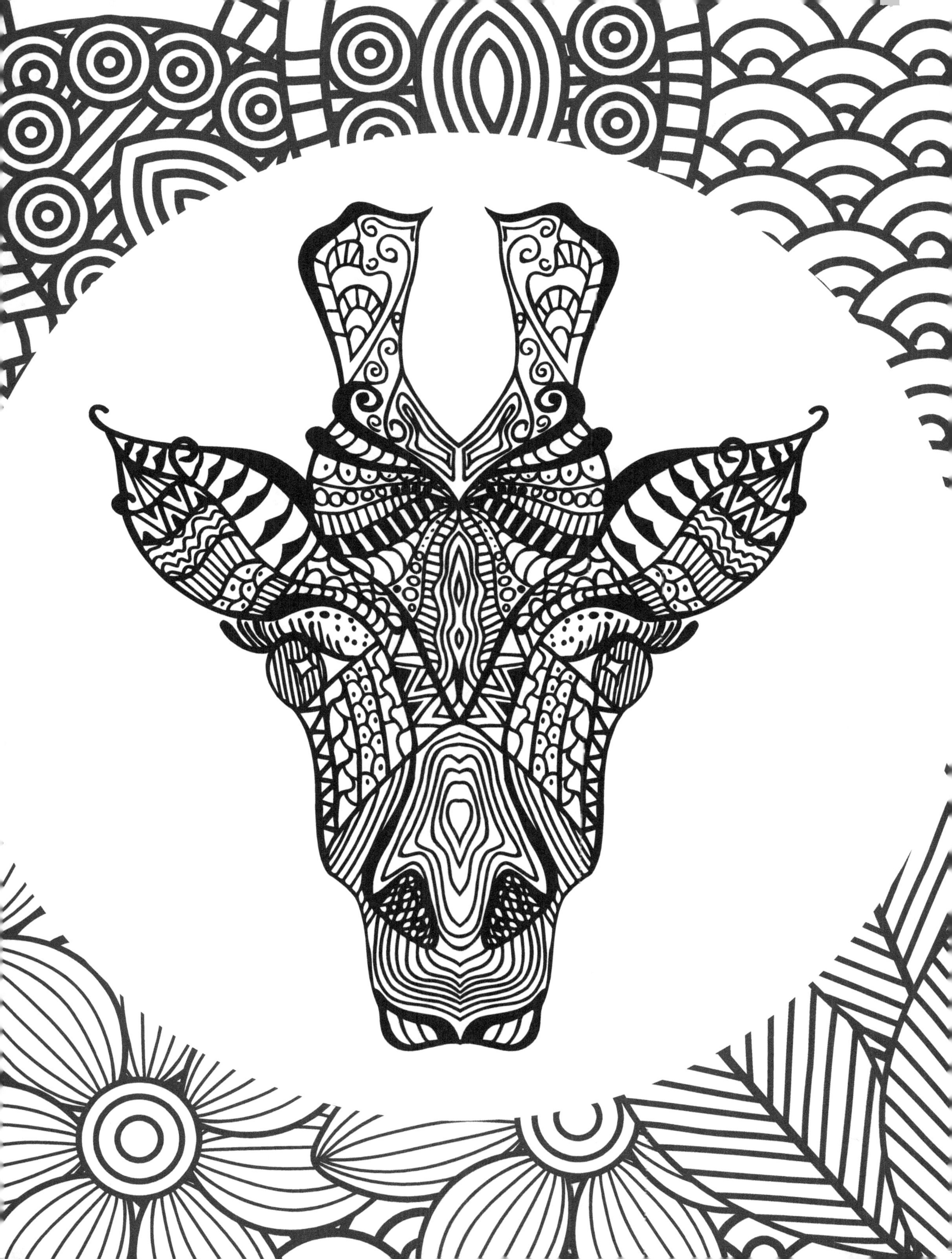

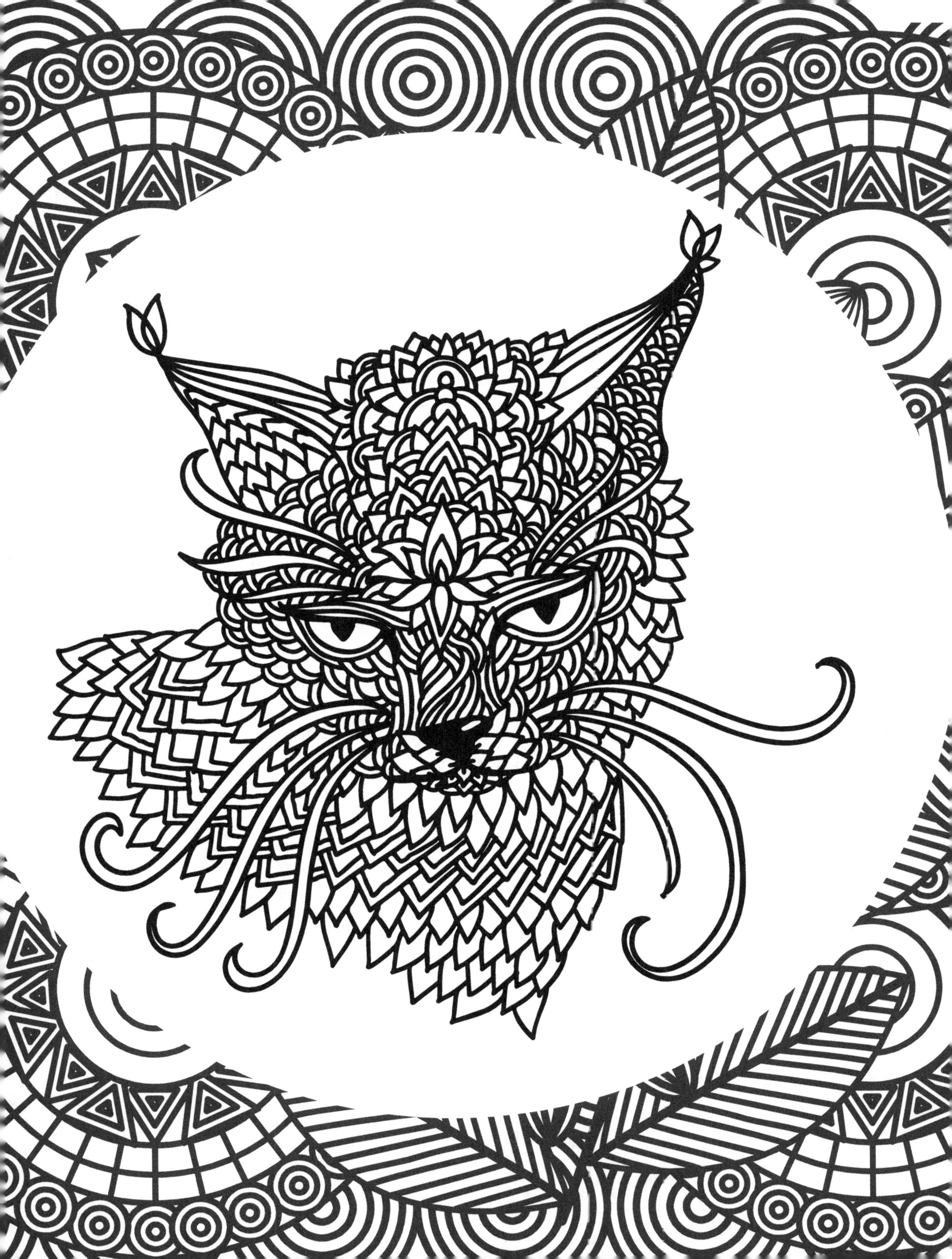

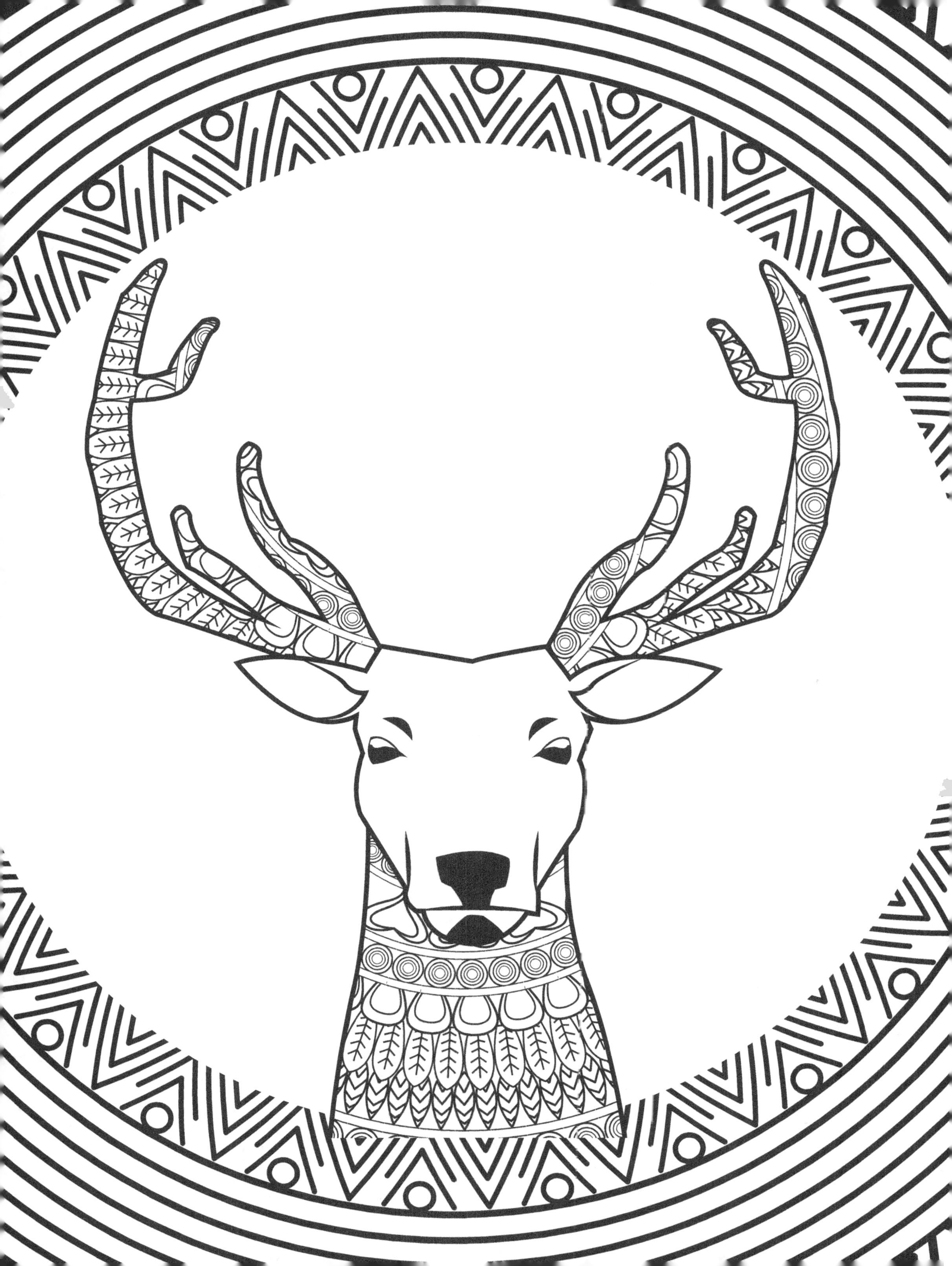

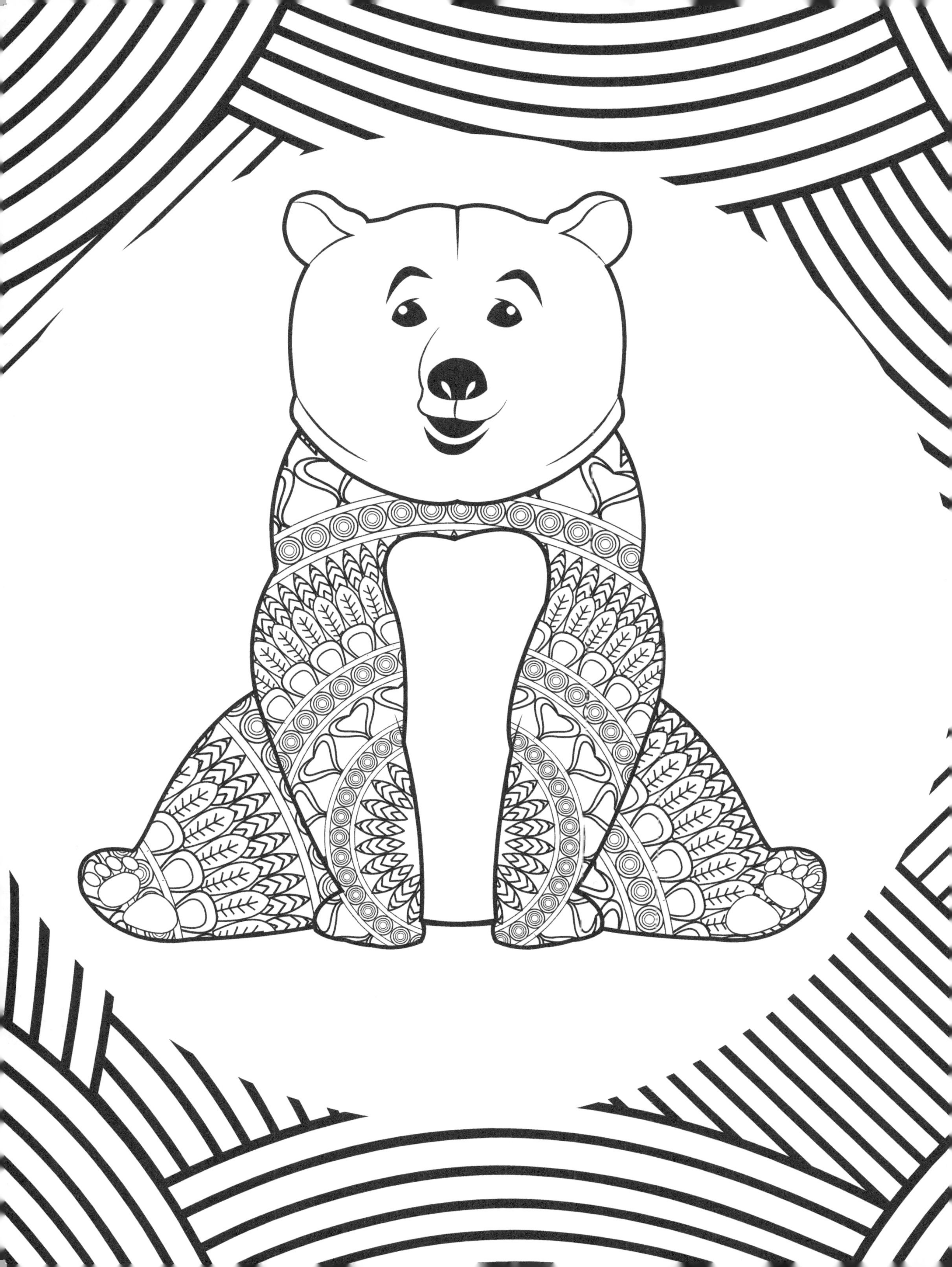

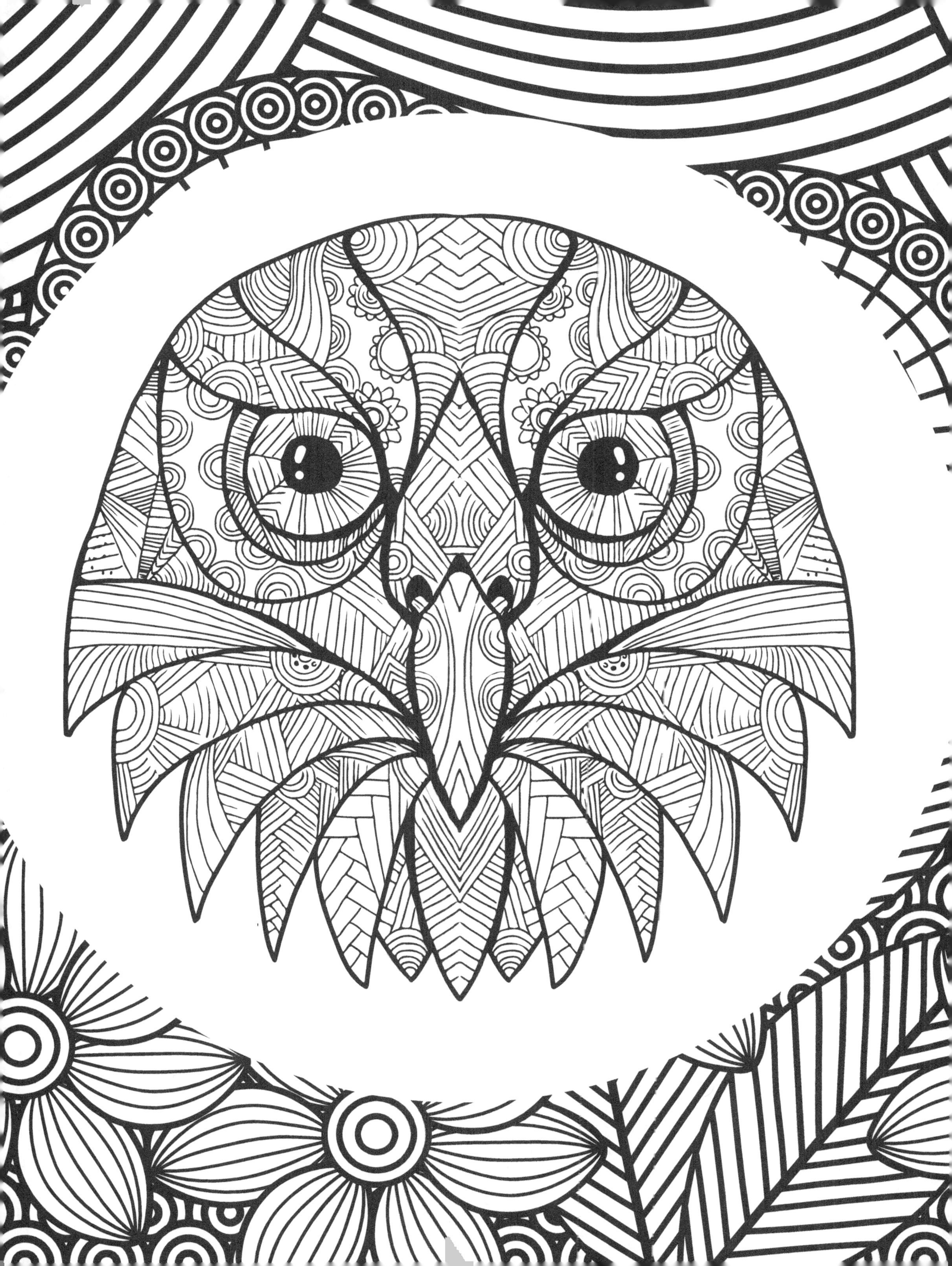

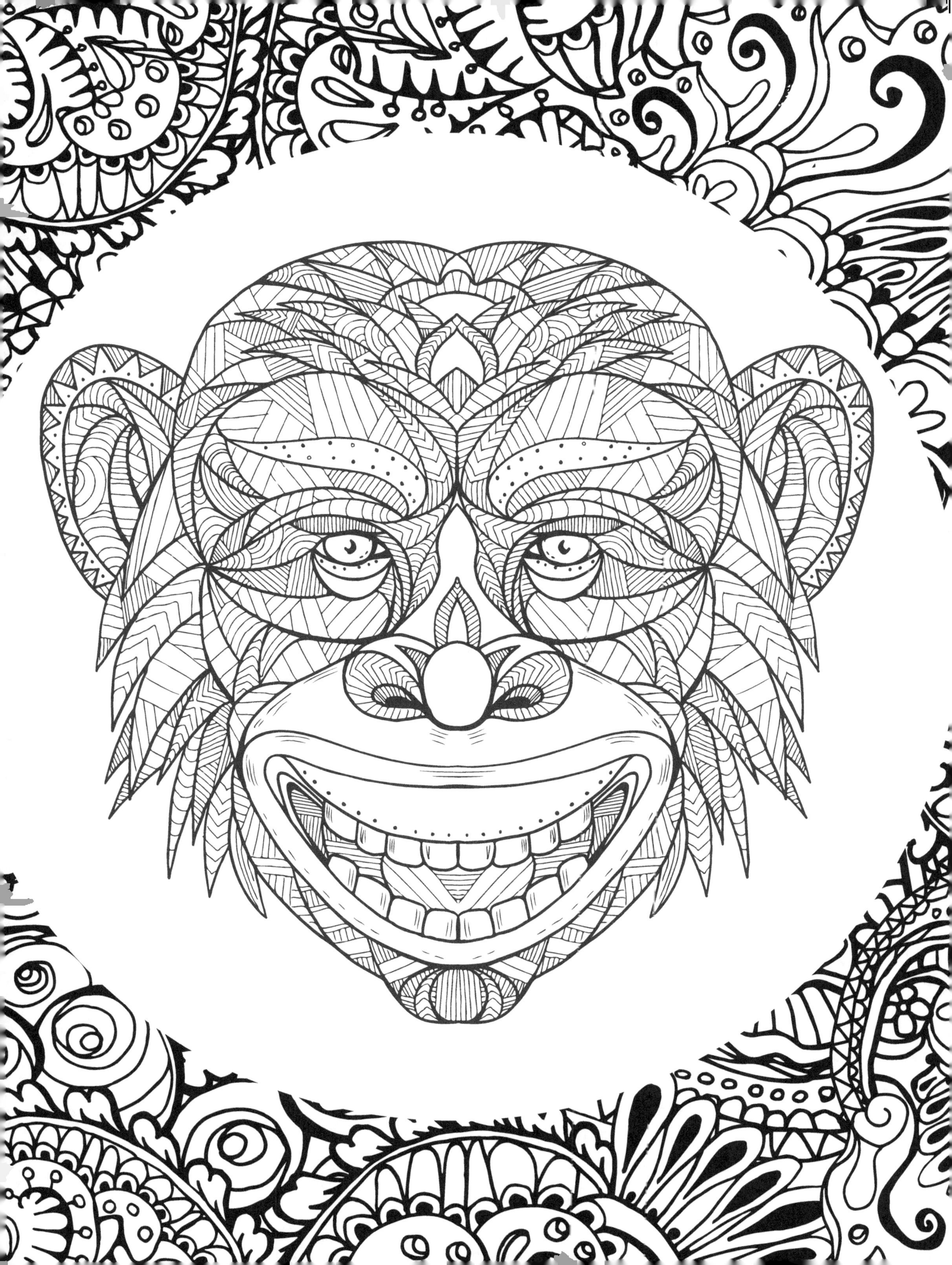

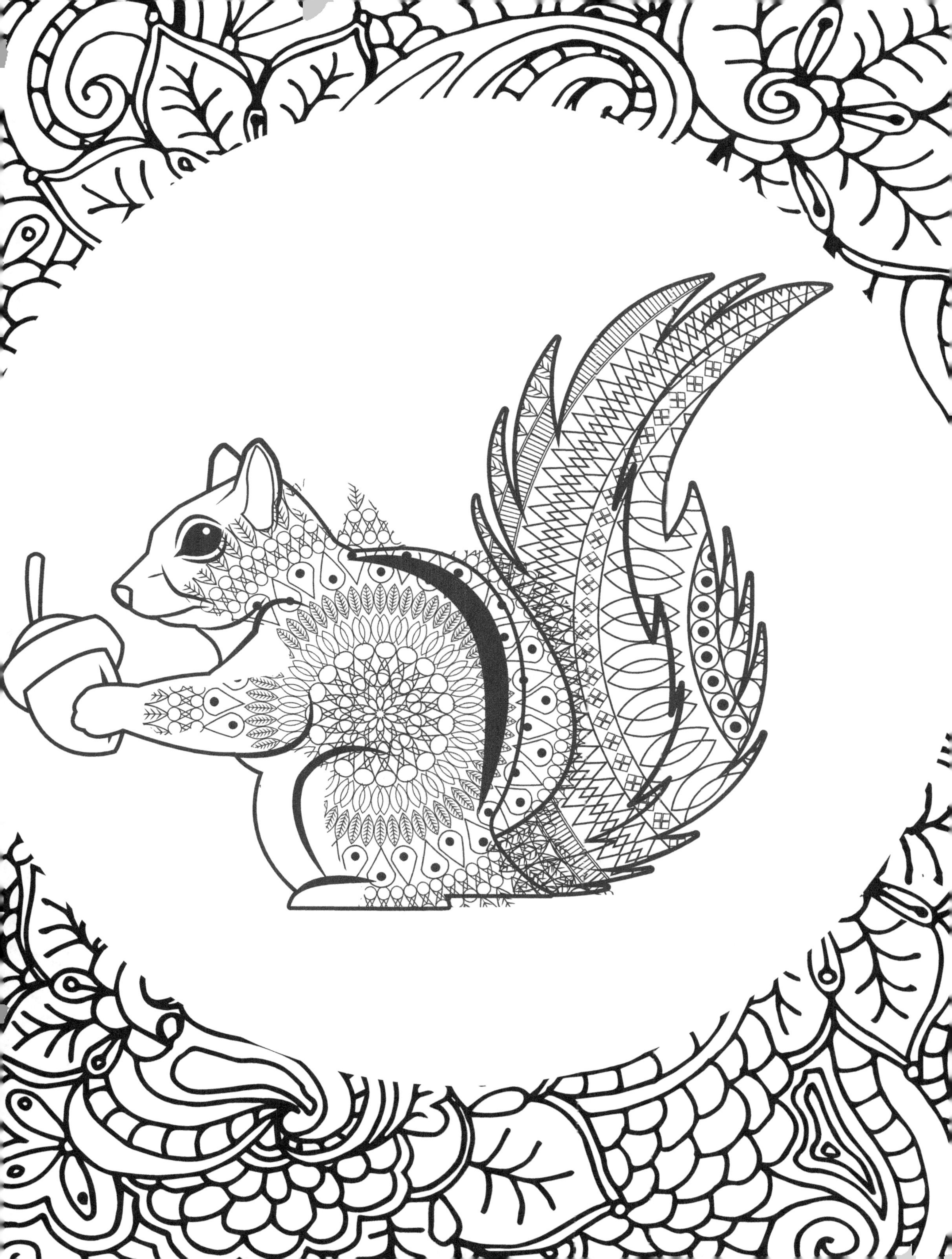

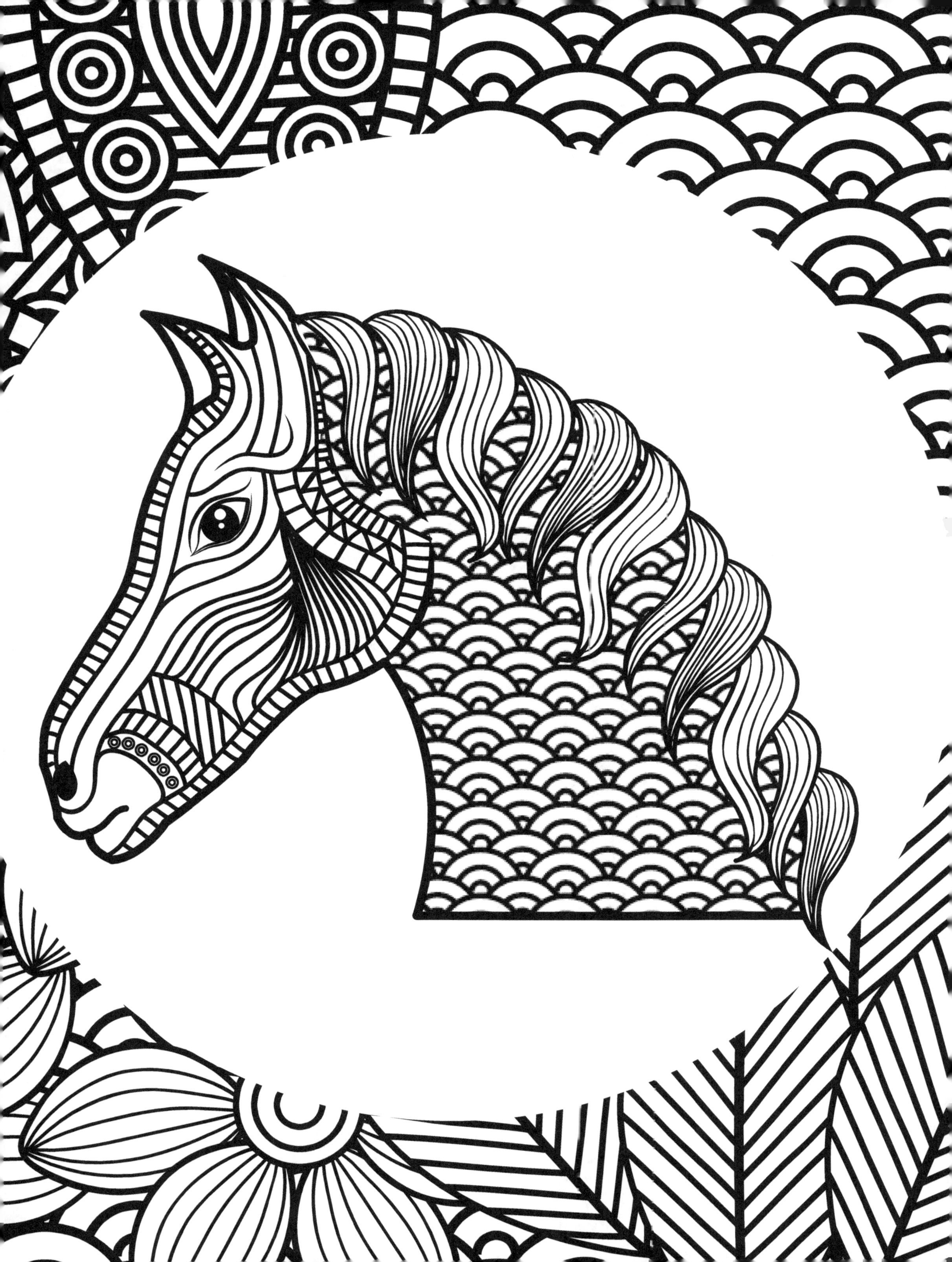

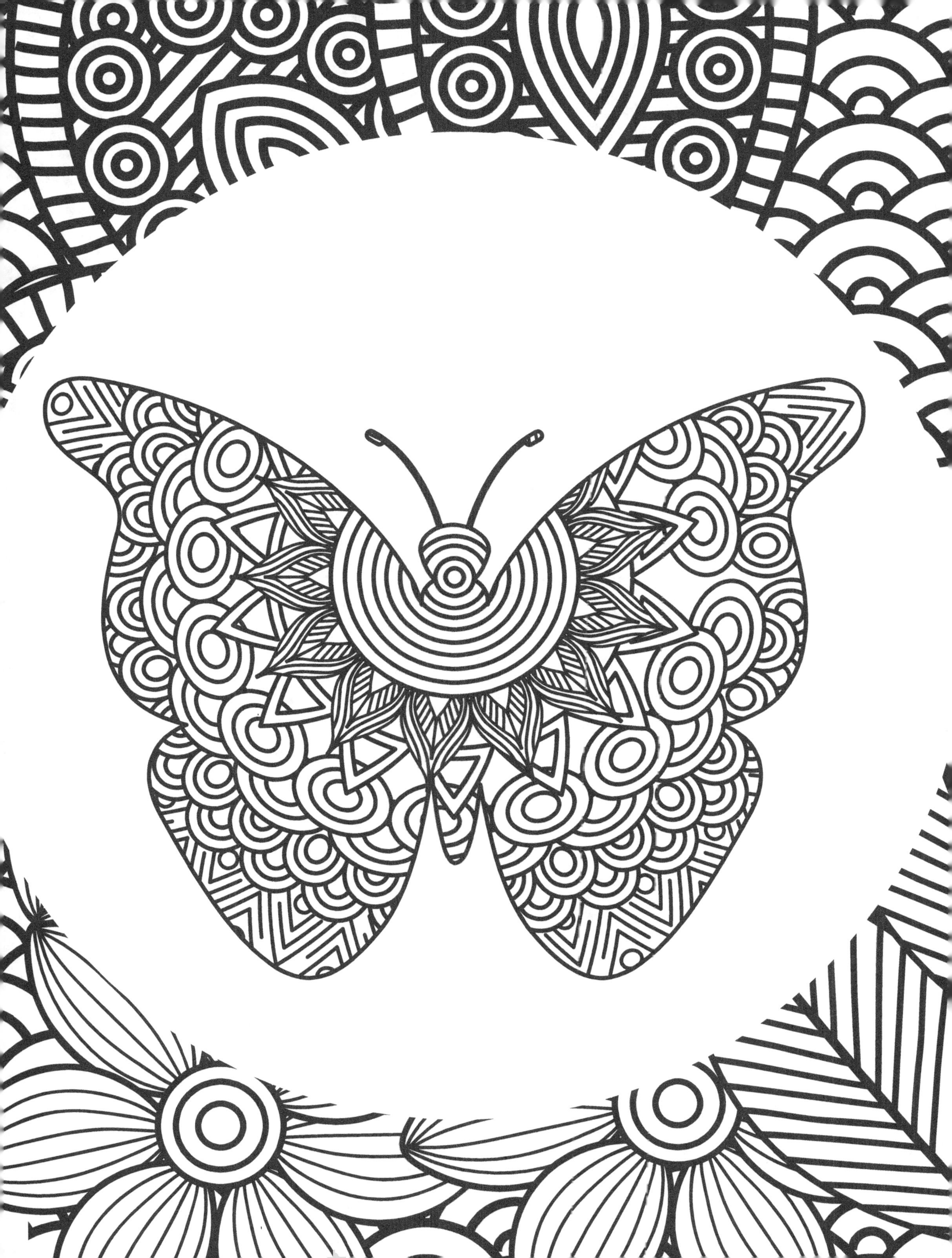

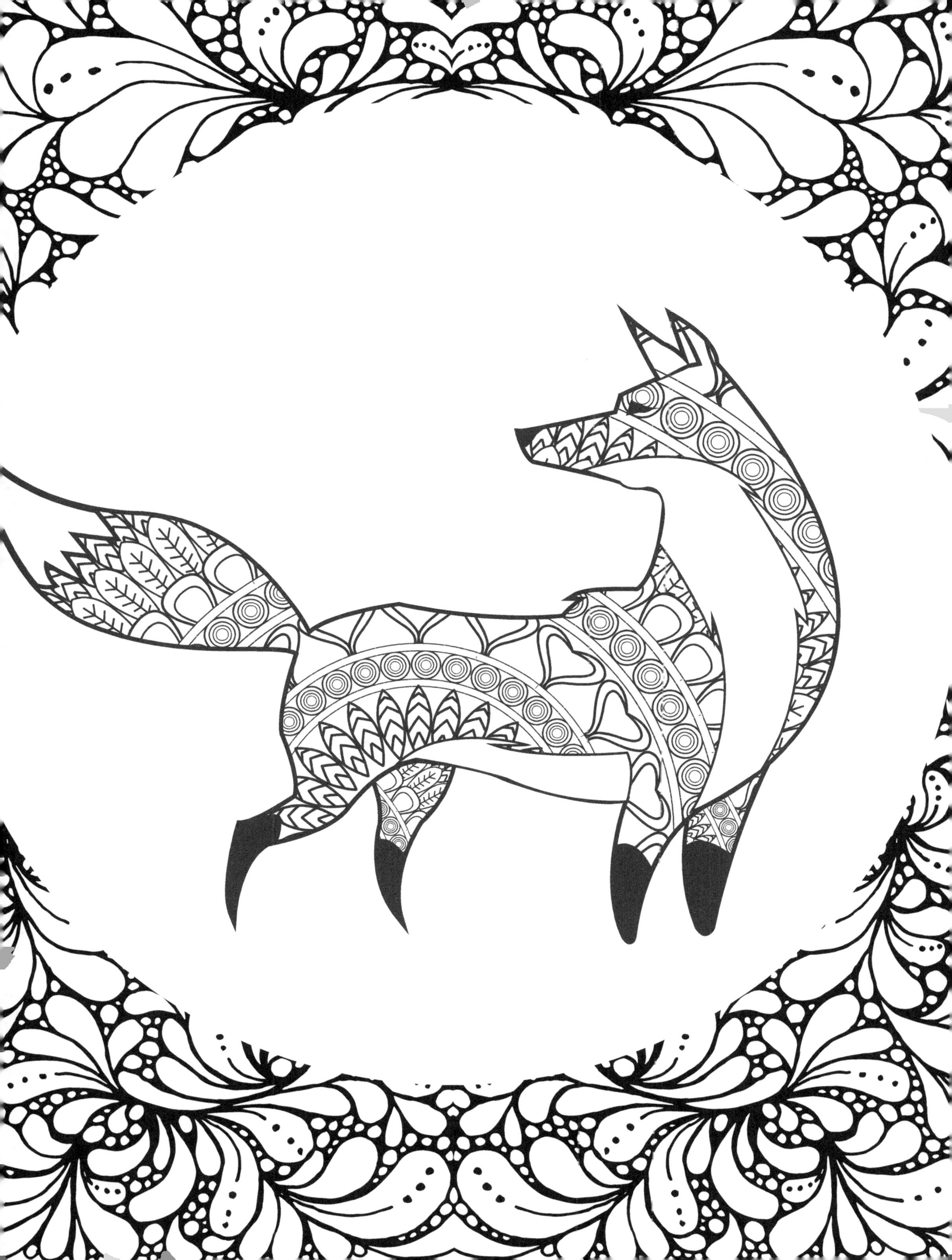

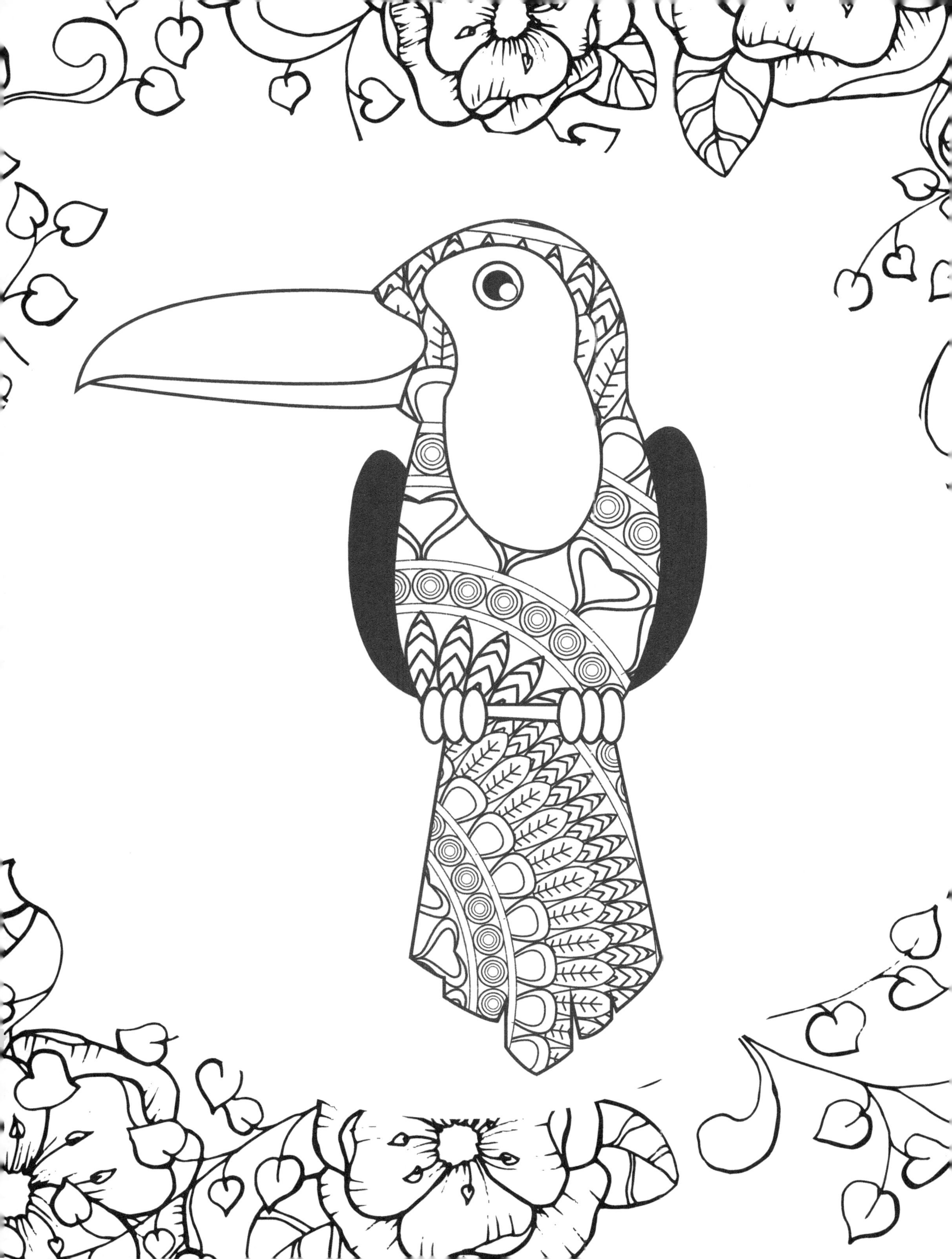

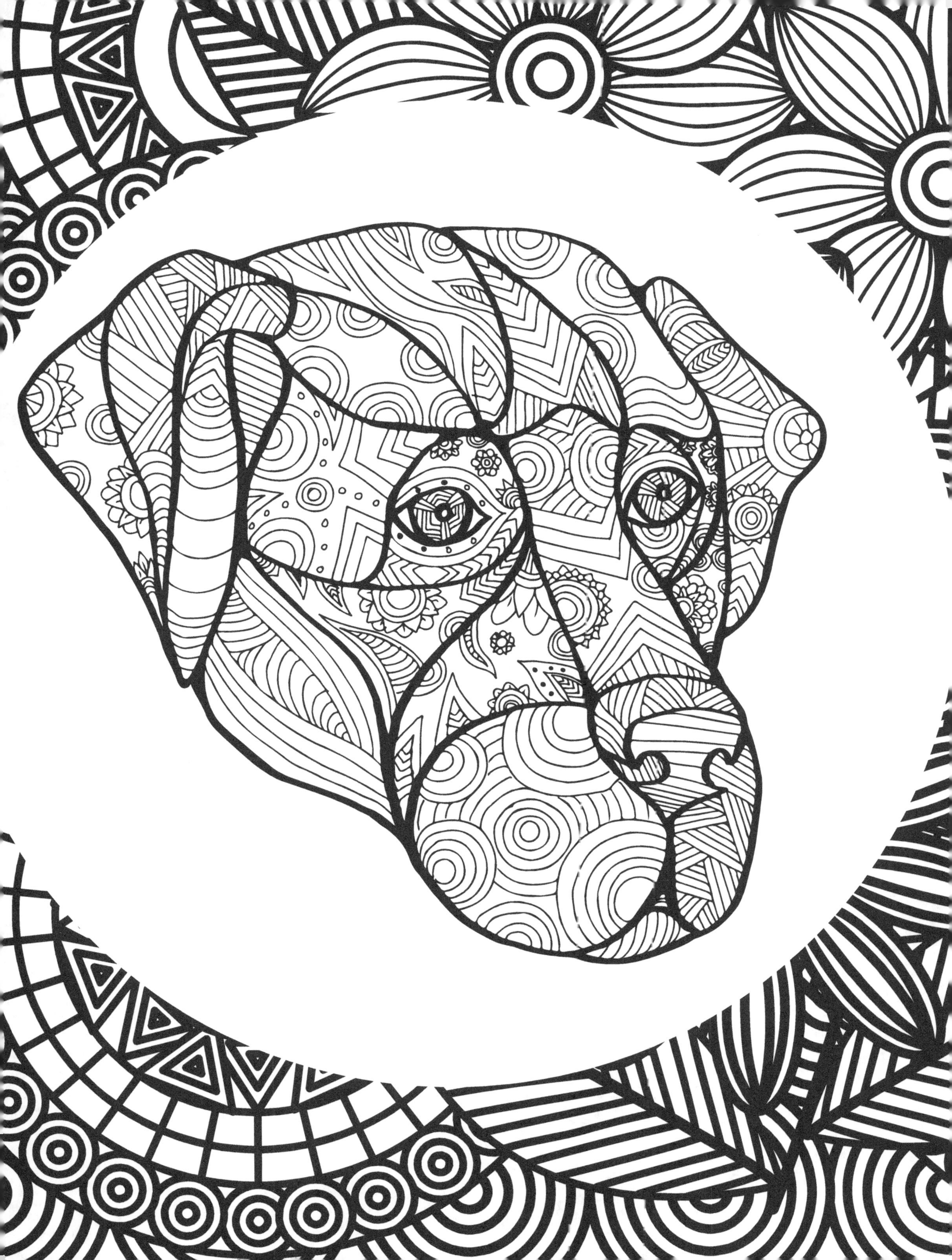

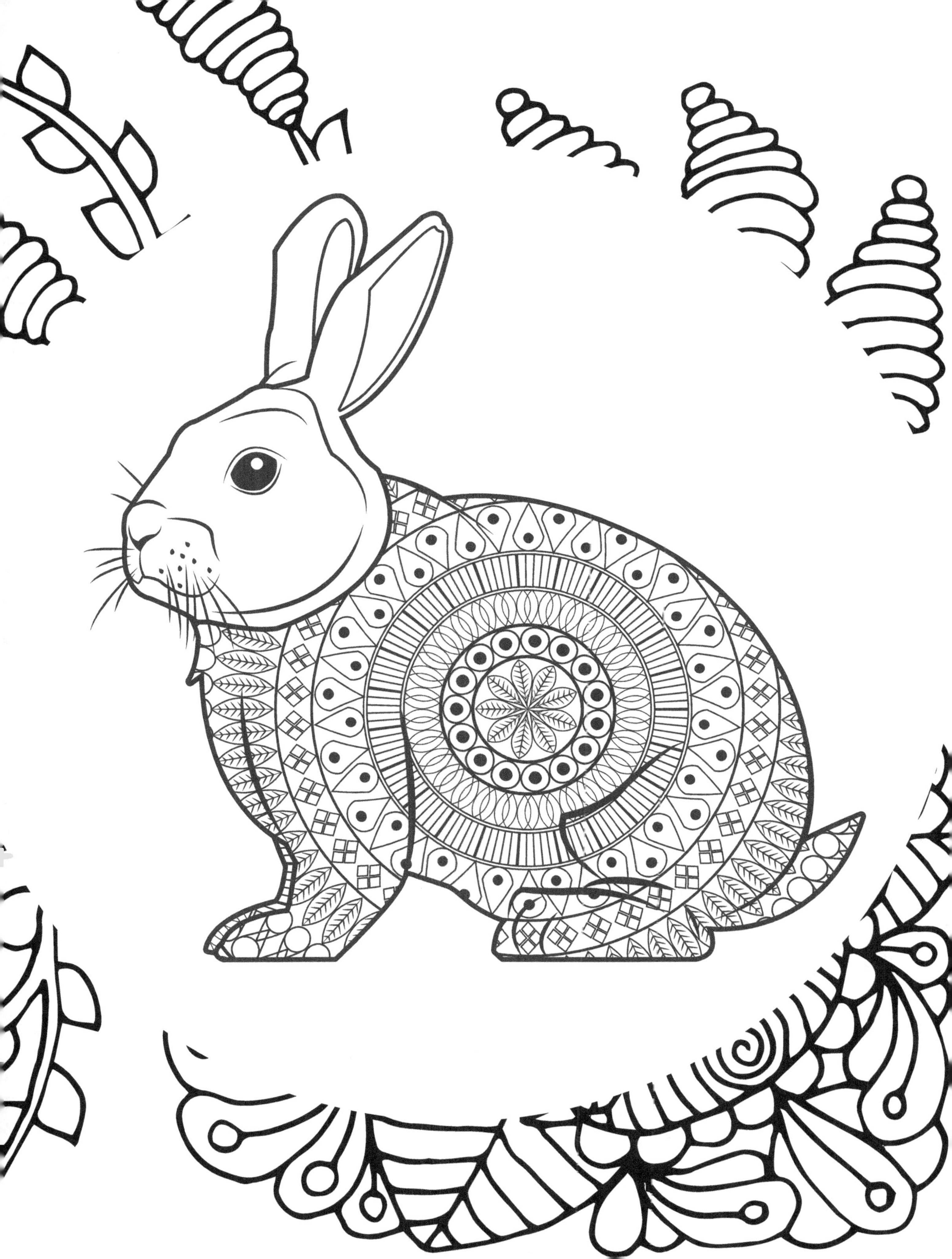

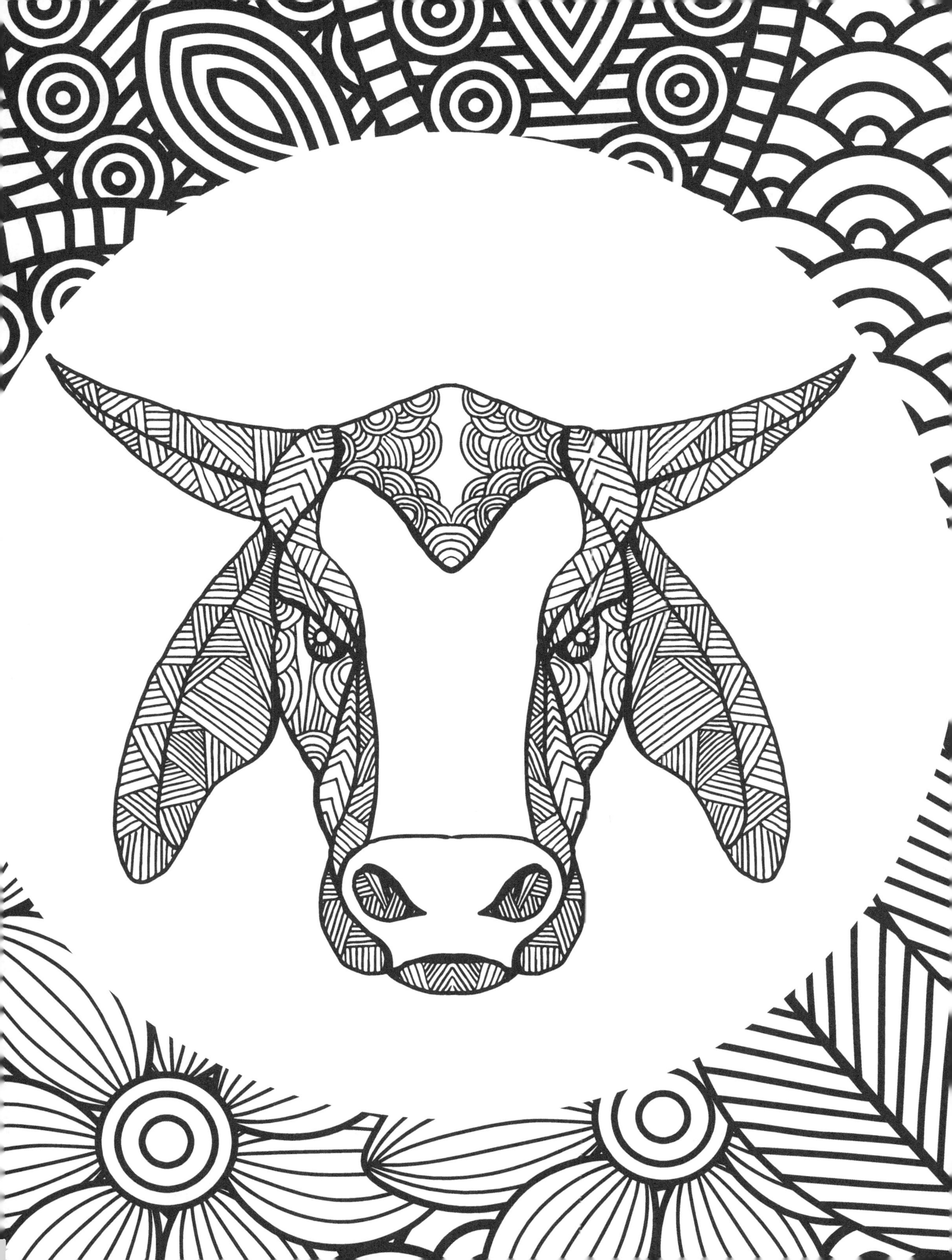

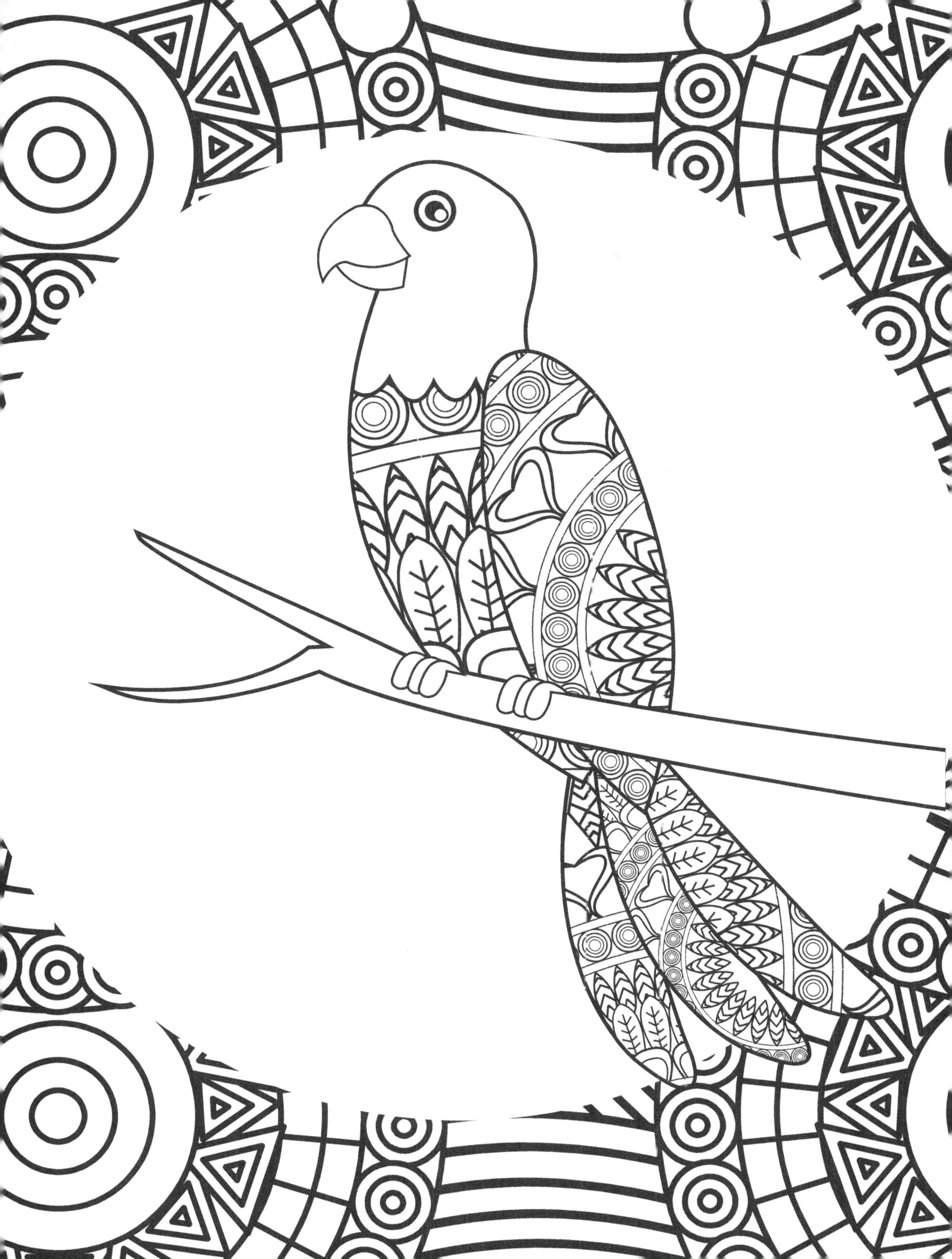

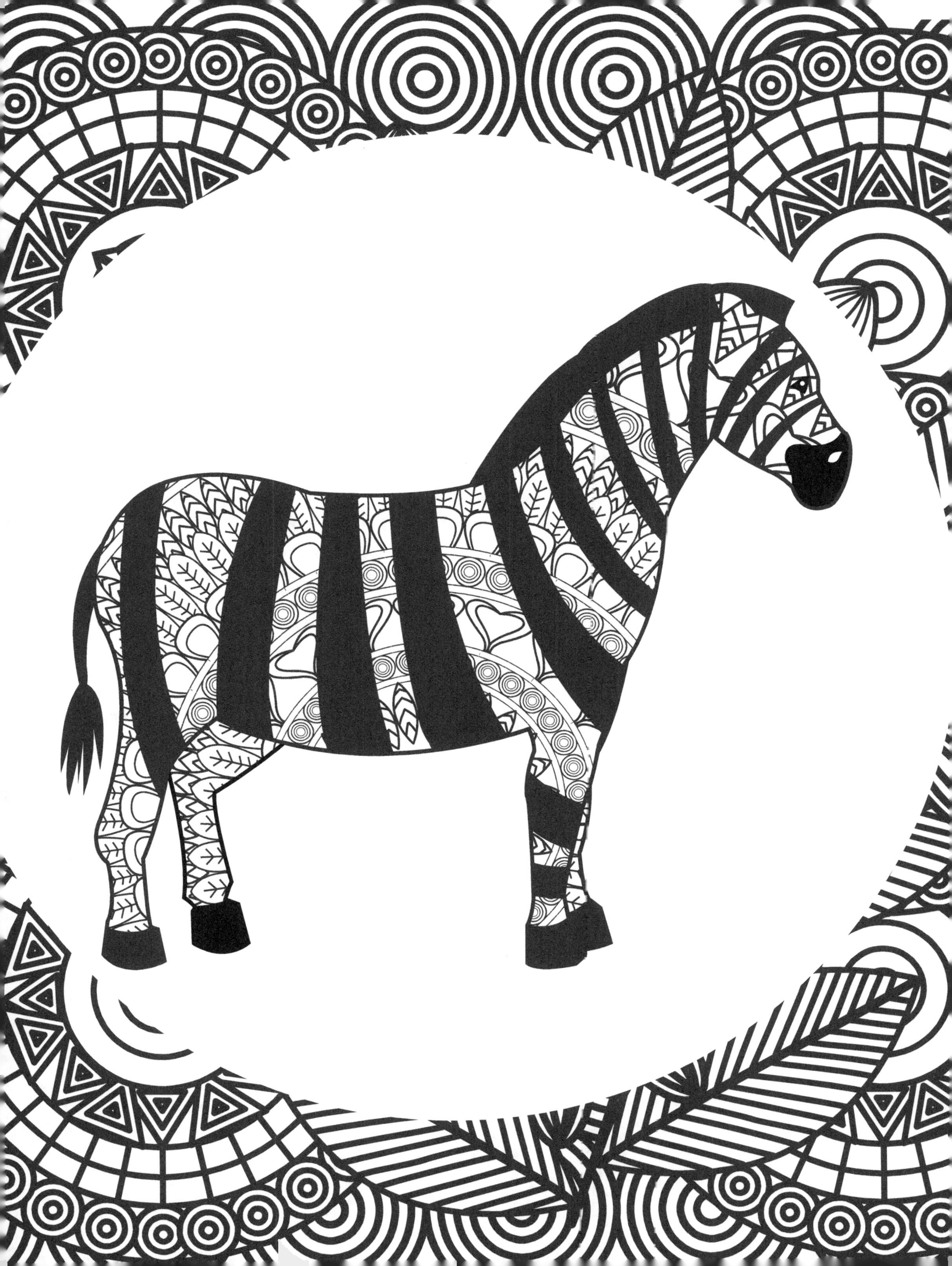

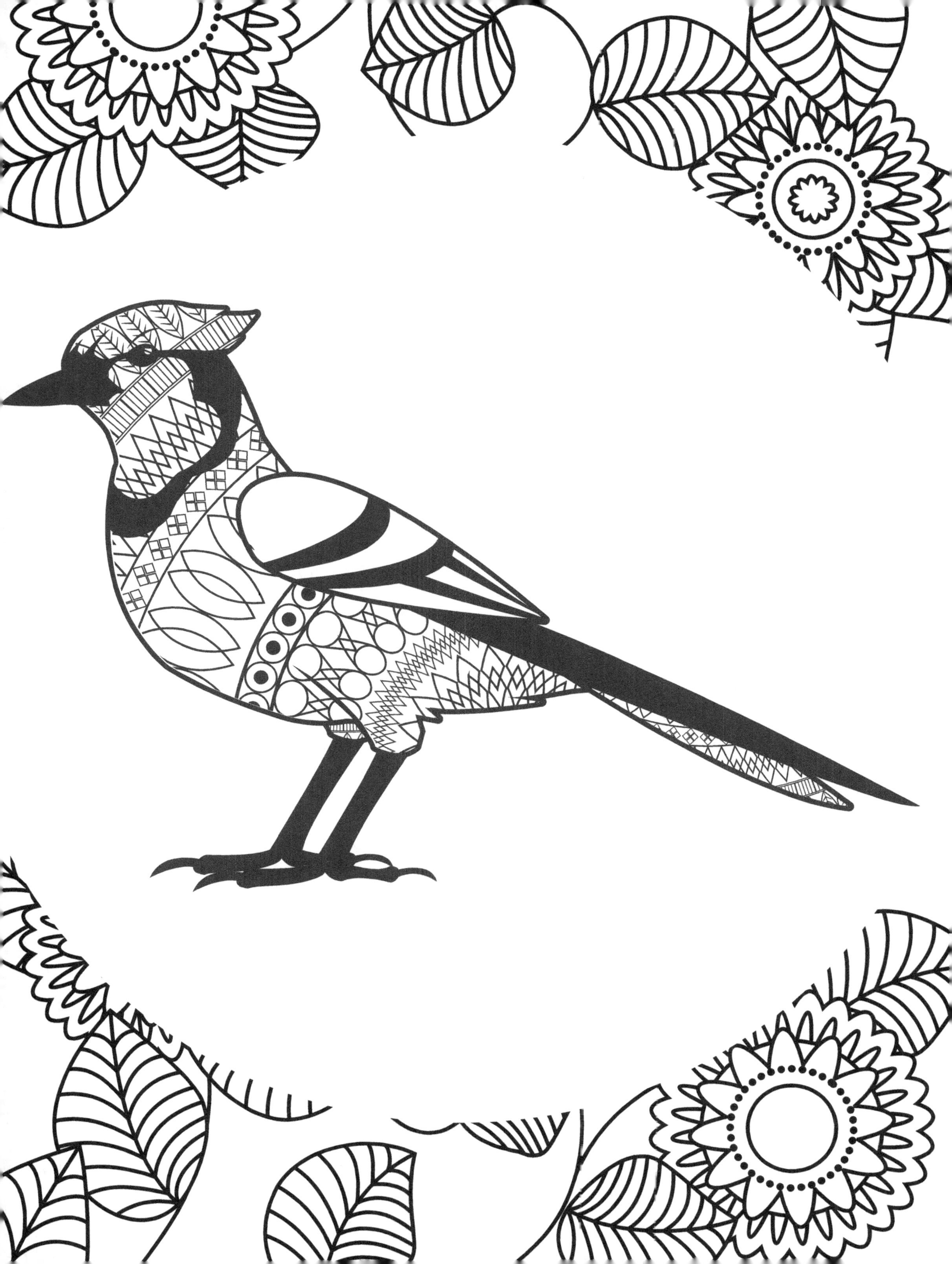

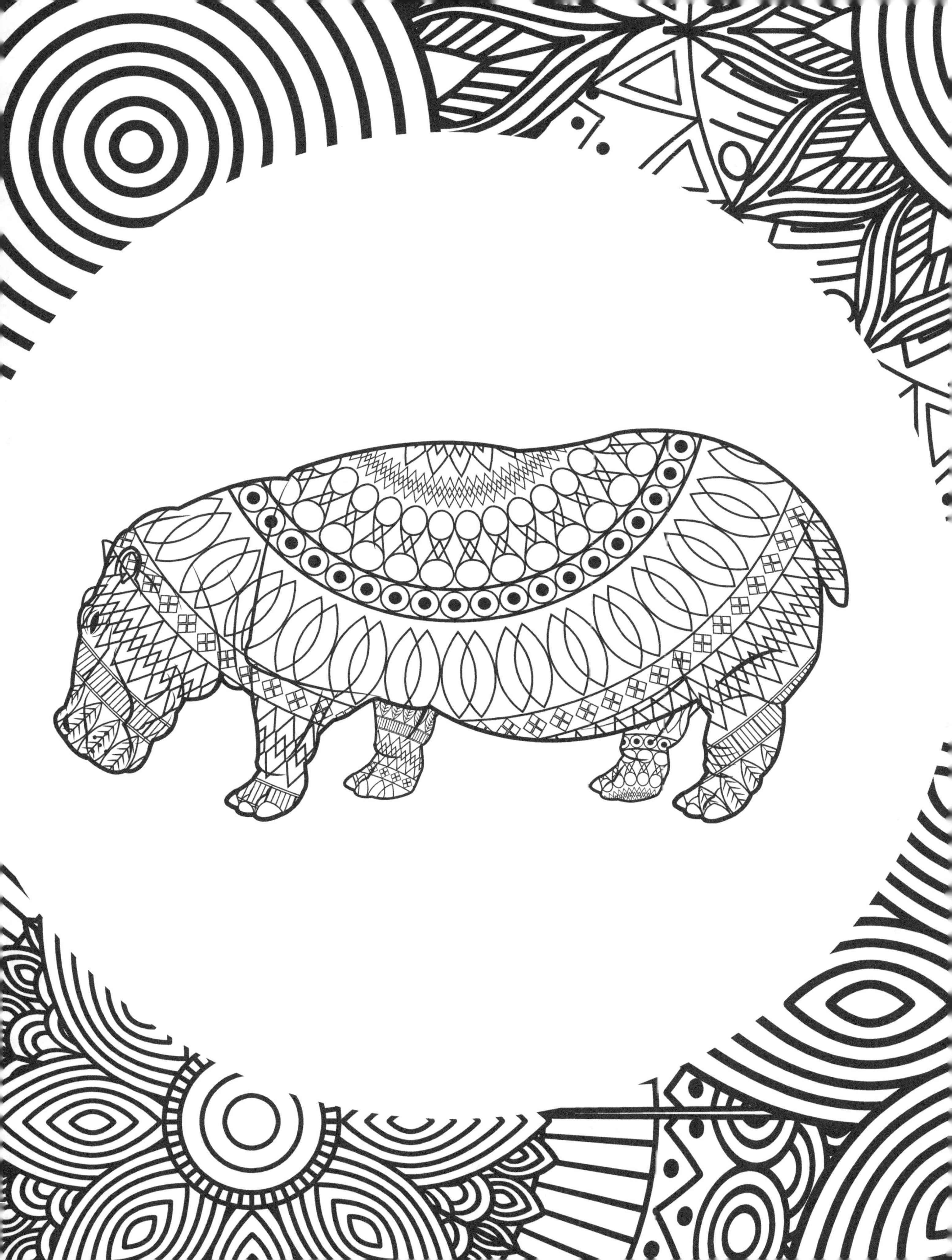

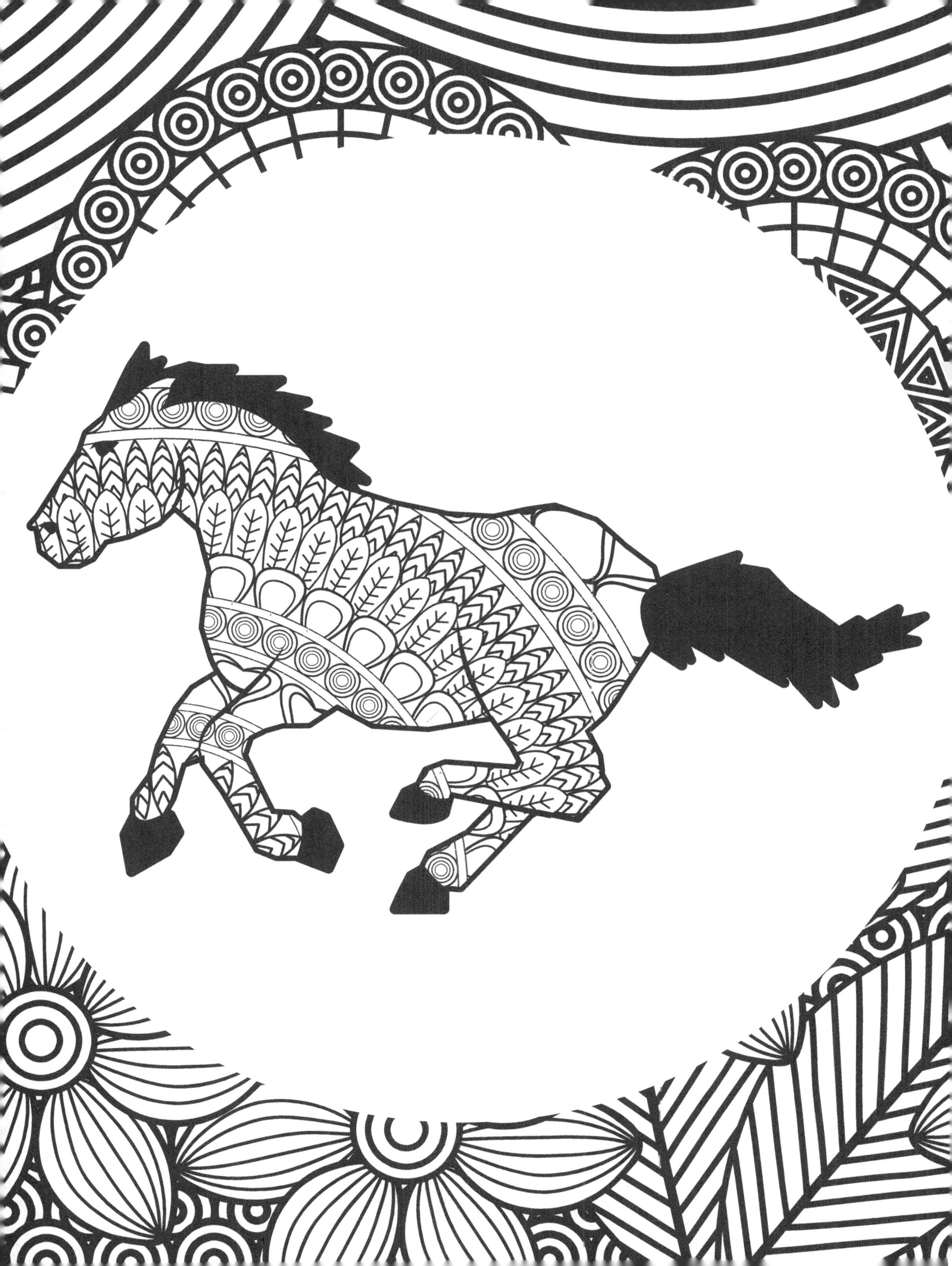

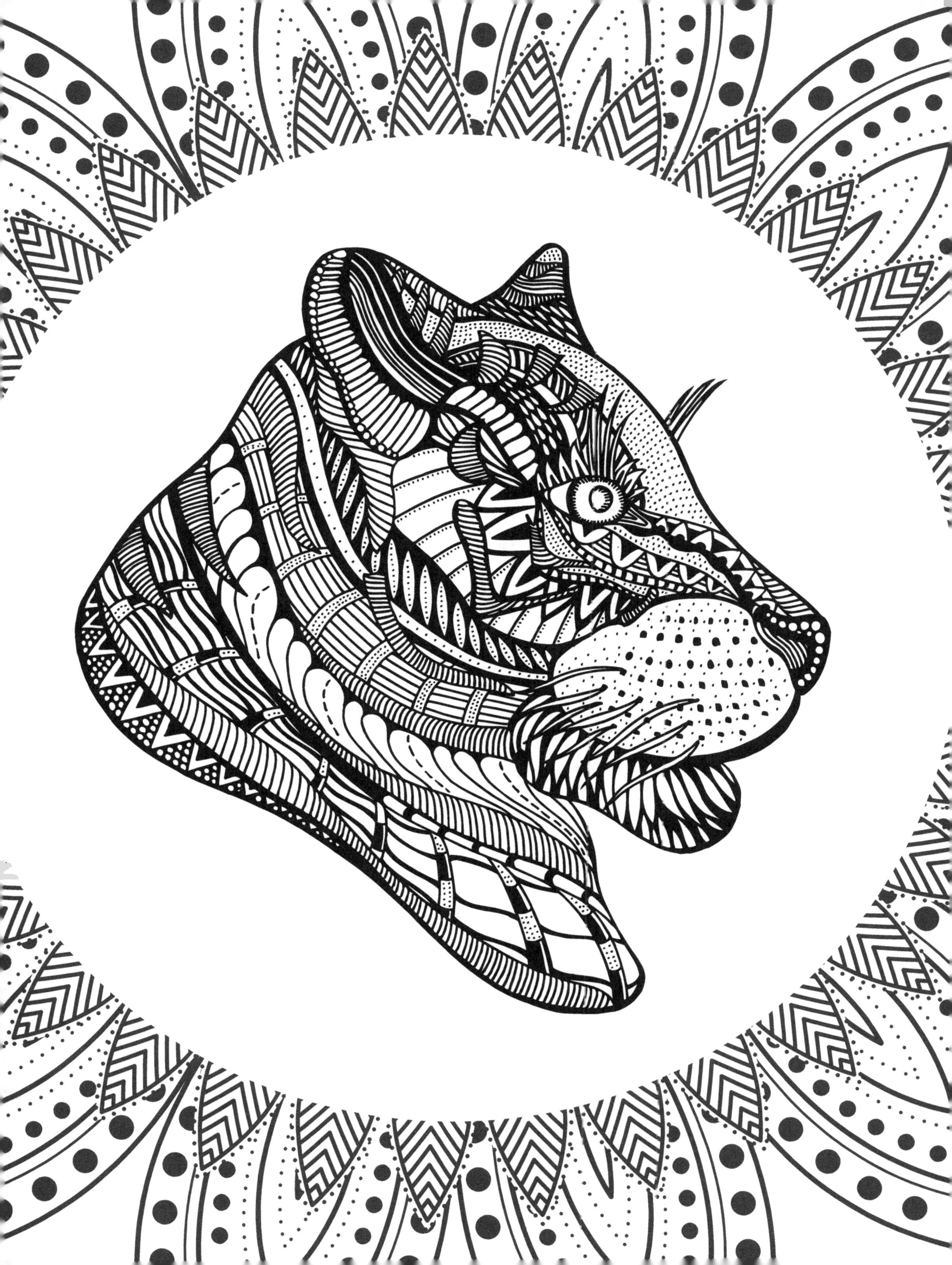

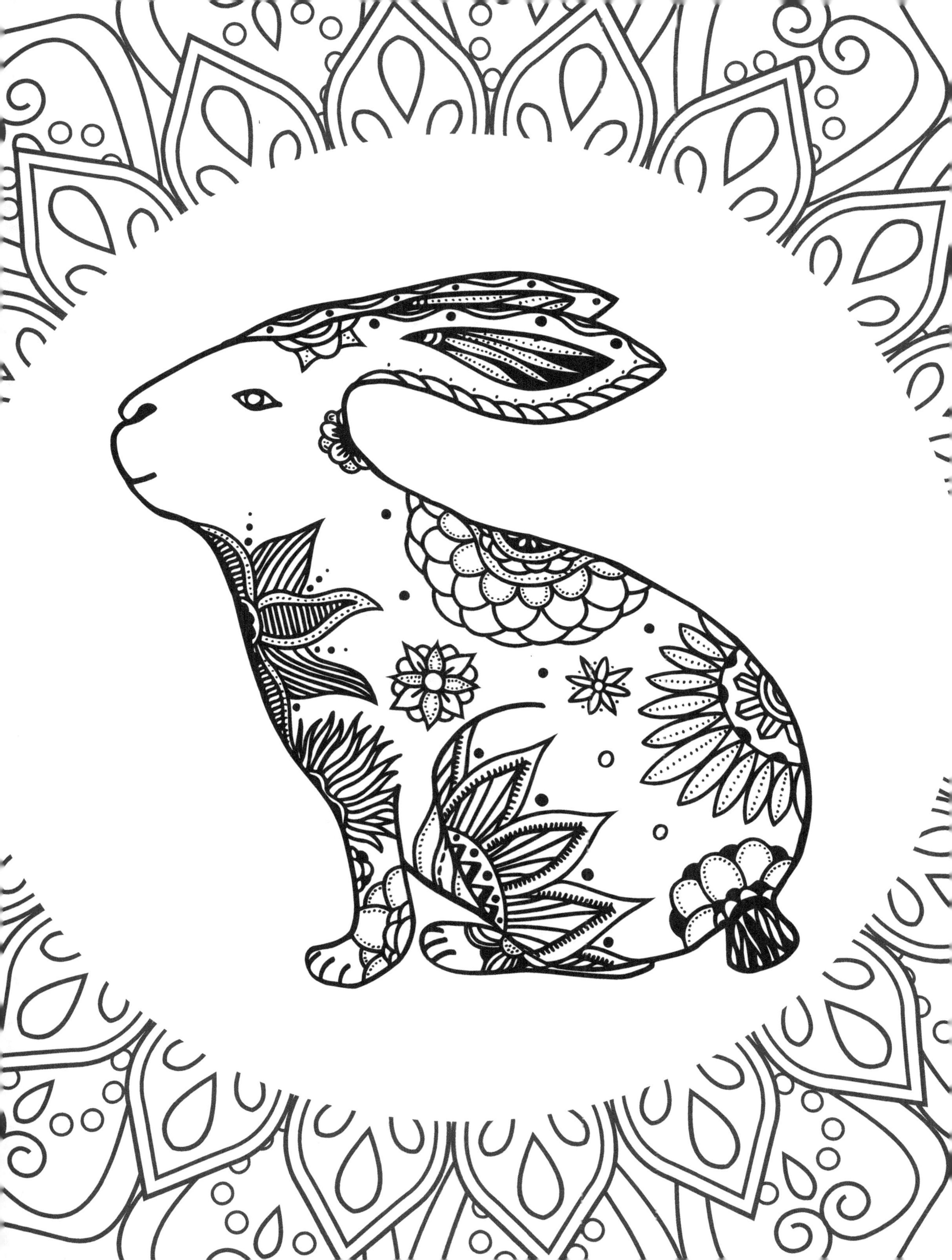

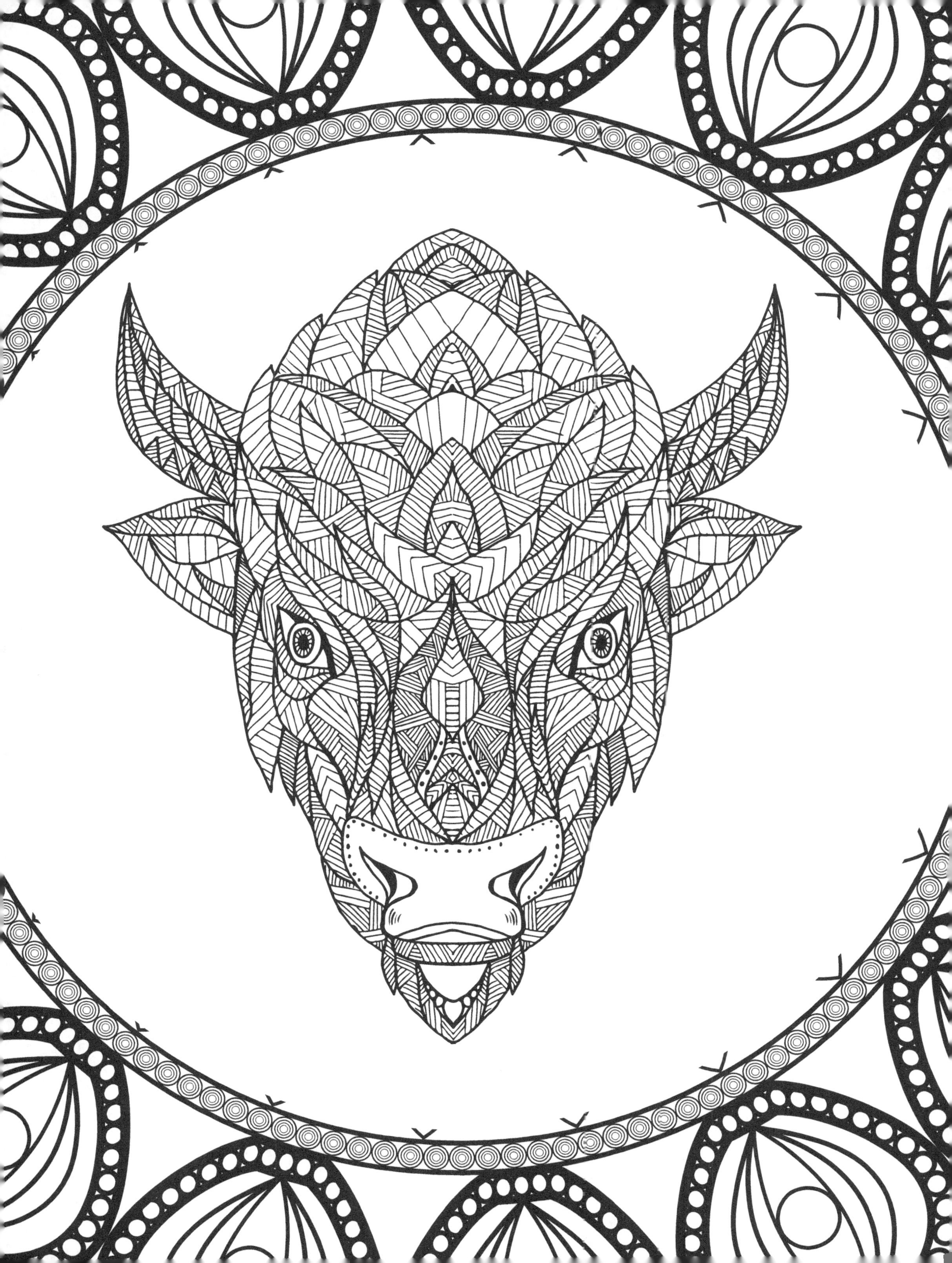

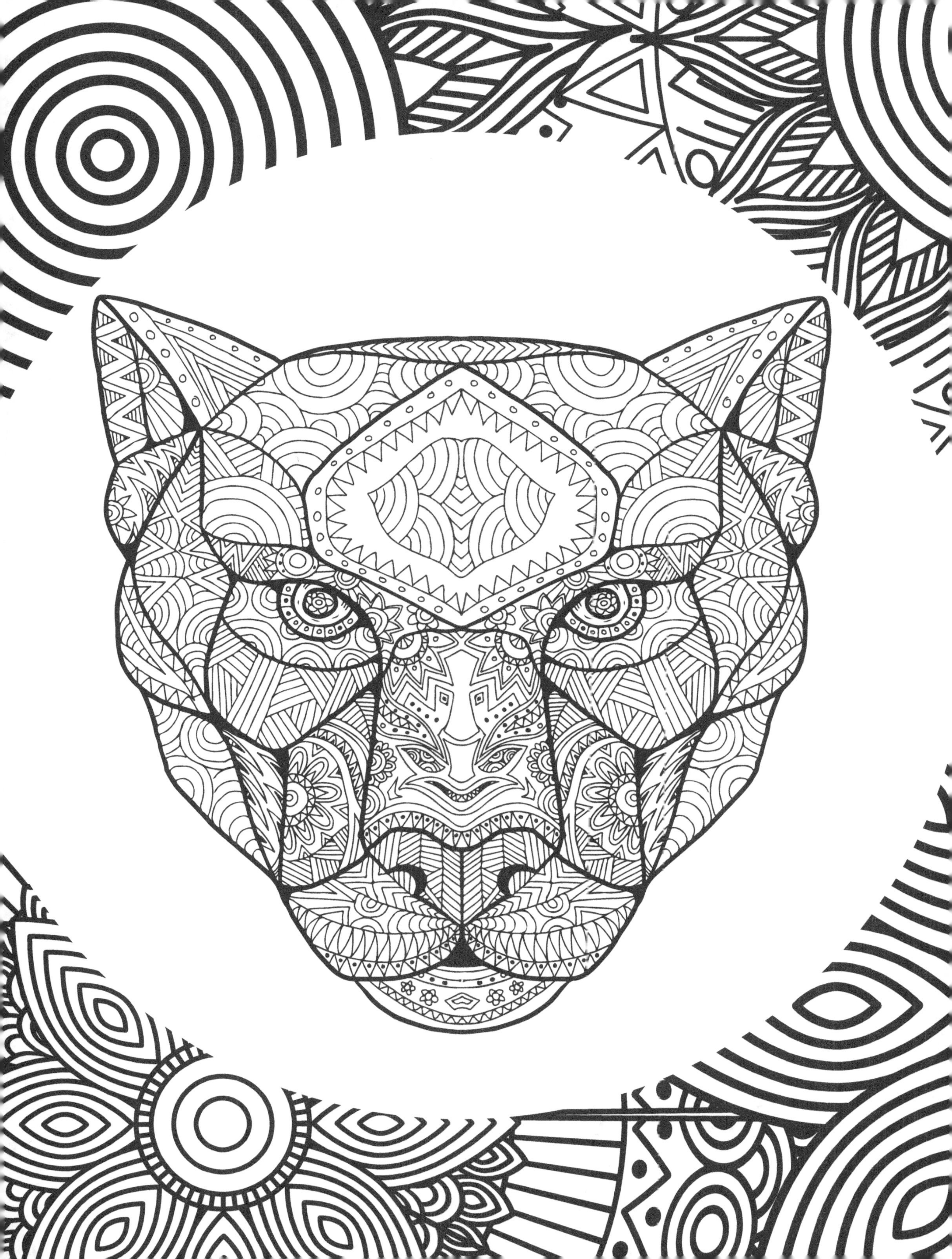

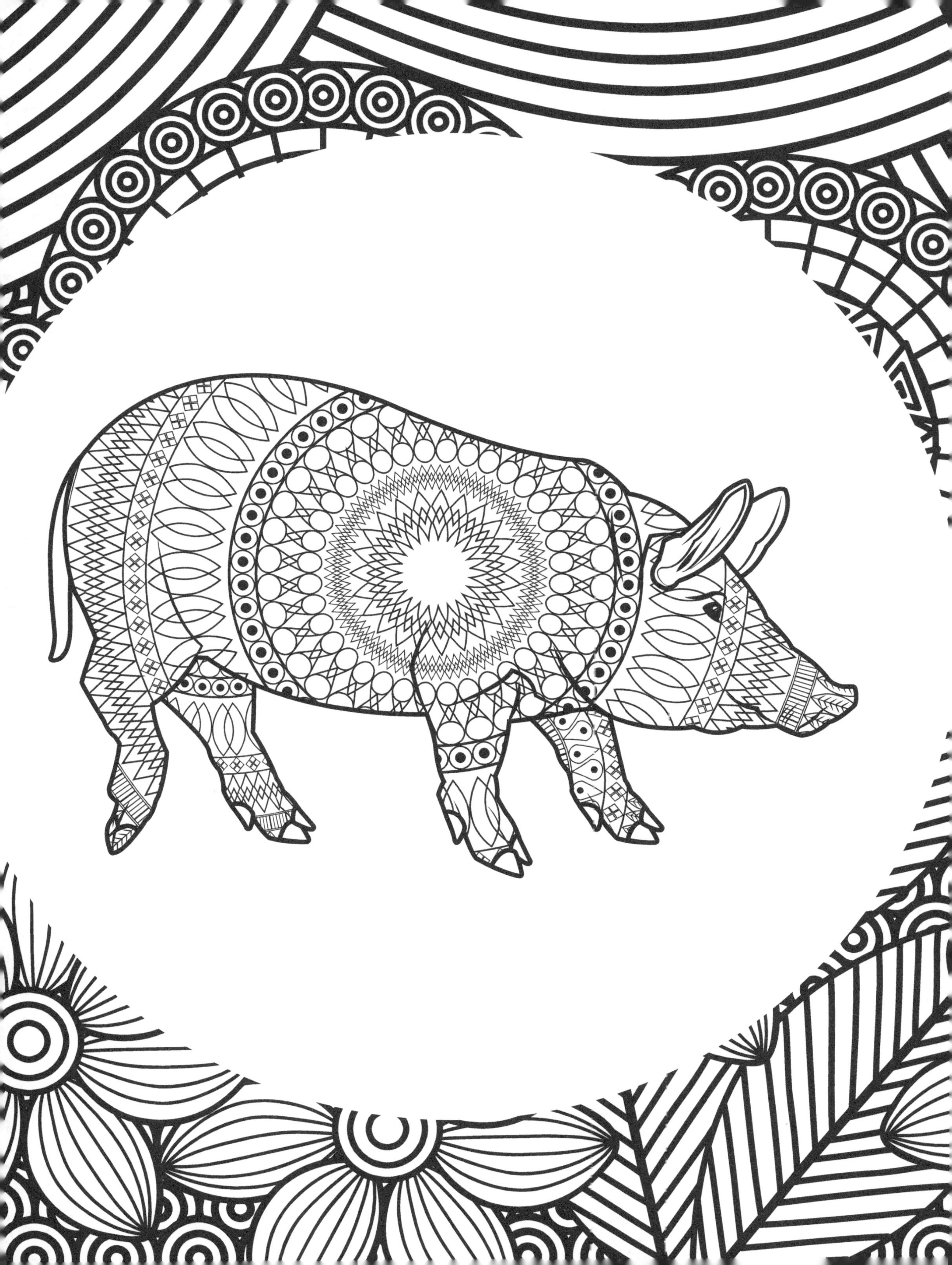

# The End

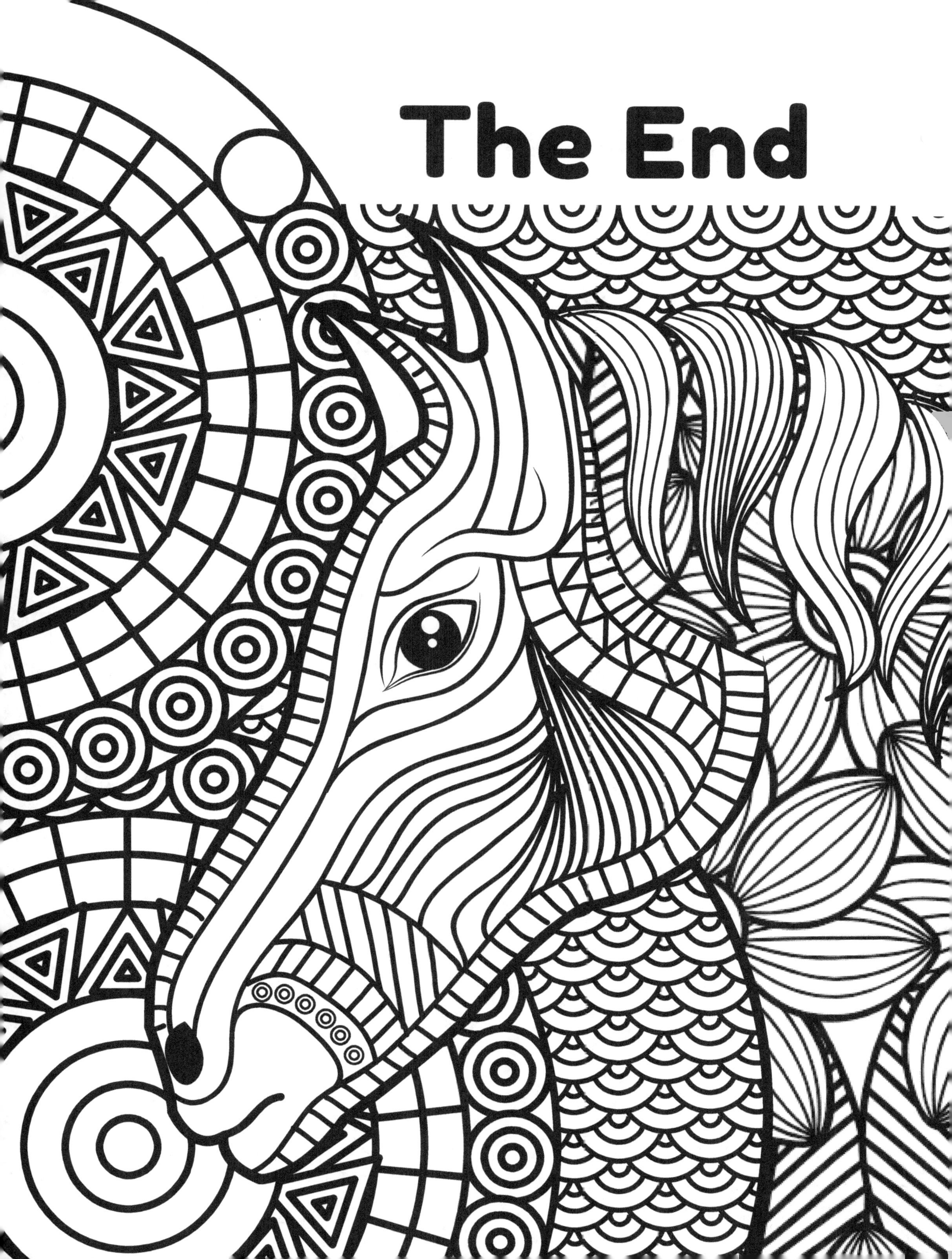